The Wild Book

The Wild Book

MARGARITA ENGLE

HARCOURT CHILDREN'S BOOKS
Houghton Mifflin Harcourt
Boston • New York • 2012

Harcourt is an imprint of Houghton Mifflin Harcourt Publishing Company.
www.hmhbooks.com
Text set in 12-point Lomba
Library of Congress Cataloging-in-Publication Data
Engle, Margarita.
The wild book / Margarita Engle.
p. cm.
Summary: In early twentieth-century Cuba, bandits terrorize the
countryside as a young farm girl struggles with dyslexia. Based on the life
of the author's grandmother.
ISBN 978-0-547-58131-6
[1. Novels in verse. 2. Dyslexia—Fiction. 3. Cuba—History—1909–1933—
Fiction.] I. Title.
PZ7.5.E54Wi 2012
[Fic]—dc23
2011027320
Manufactured in the United States of America
DOC 10 9 8 7 6 5 4 3 2
4500356828

For young readers
who dread reading

and for those
who love blank books

Mis ojos miraban en hora de ensueños

      la página blanca.

Y vino el desfile de ensueños y sombras.

In the hour of daydreams my eyes watched

      the blank page.

And there came a parade of dreams and shadows.

      —Rubén Darío,

         from "La Página Blanca" ("The Blank Page")

The Cuban Countryside

1912

Word-Blindness

Word-blindness.
The doctor hisses it
like a curse.
Word-blindness,
he repeats—some children
can see everything
except words.
They are only blind
on paper.
Fefa will never be able
to read, or write,
or be happy
in school.

Word-blindness.
It sounds like an evil wizard's
prophecy, dangerous
and dreadful,
but Mamá does not listen

to the serpent voice
of the hissing doctor.
She climbs in the wagon,
clucks to the horse,
and carries us home
to our beautiful green farm,
where she tells me to follow
the good example of Santa Mónica,
patron saint of patience.

Word-blindness,
Mamá murmurs
with a suffering sigh—who
ever heard of such an impossible
burden?

She refuses to accept
the hissing doctor's verdict.
Seeds of learning grow slowly,
she assures me.
Then she lights a tall,

slender candle,
and gives me
a book.

I grow anxious.
I pretend that my eyes hurt.
I pretend that my head hurts,
and pretty soon
it is true.

I know that the words
want to trick me.
The letters will jumble
and spill off the page,
leaping and hopping,
jumping far away,
like slimy
bullfrogs.

Think of this little book
as a garden,

Mamá suggests.
She says it so calmly
that I promise I will try.

Throw wildflower seeds
all over each page, she advises.
Let the words sprout
like seedlings,
then relax and watch
as your wild diary
grows.

6

I open the book.
Word-blindness.
The pages are white!
Is this really a blank diary,
or just an ordinary
schoolbook
filled with frog-slippery
tricky letters
that know how to leap
and escape?

School

The others laugh.
They always laugh.
When I am forced to read
OUT LOUD,
they mock
my stumbling voice,
and when I have to practice
my horrible
handwriting,
they make fun
of the twisted
tilted
tormented
letters.

My fingers fall away
from the page.
I lose the courage
to try.

Homework

I struggle to write
in my blank book,
my wild diary,
just a little bit
each evening
by candlelight.

It is almost impossible
to practice patiently!

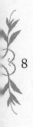

I hate hate hate
this deep dread
of slippery
vanishing words
that make me feel
so lonely.

Frog Fear

My little brothers love
to frighten me
by hiding lizards,
bugs, and spiders
in my bloomers.

Today it's a frog,
but they tell me it's a snake,
so I scream and tremble
until I can clearly see
that the little creature
jumps around
like jittery letters
on a blinding
page.

The skin of a frog
feels just as slippery
and tricky as a wild
inky word.

9

Homework Fear

The teacher at school
smiles, but she's too busy
to give me extra help,
so later, at home,
Mamá tries to teach me.

She reminds me
to go oh-so-slowly
and take my time.
There is no hurry.
The heavy book
will not rise up
and fly away.

When I scramble the sneaky letters
b and *d*, or the even trickier ones
r and *l*, Mamá helps me learn
how to picture
the sep—a—rate
parts

of each mys—te—ri—ous
syl—la—ble.
Still, it's not easy
to go so
ss—ll—oo—ww—ll—yy.
S l o w l y.
SLOWLY!

I have to keep
warning myself
over and over
that whenever I try
to read too quickly,
my clumsy patience
flips over
and tumbles,
then falls . . .

Why?
Wwhhyyyy?
WHY?
¡Ay!

Word Towers

Listen listen listen.
I have to learn how to listen!
Please, God, help me hear
all the mysterious sounds
of each wild word.

I watch Mamá as she cradles
a book of poems,
holding it like a baby,
with love, instead of fear.
How can reading look
so easy, and feel
so impossible?

The long poems
look like towers so tall
that I could never
hope
to climb

12

all the wispy
letters.

Words seem to float
and drift, changing
their strange shapes,
like storm clouds,
always ready
to explode.

Tiny Triumphs

I try to slow down
and really see
the little parts
that I can hear,
all those
scattered
bits
of ti—ny
words.

Will my mind
ever be ti—dy?

Will my wild book
ever seem
tame?

Lonely Fear

My big sisters go out riding
fast horses in adventurous places,
even though we should all
be at home, doing our chores.
They don't let me go with them.
They say they plan
to explore an eerie tower
on an old sugar plantation
where ghostly legends
moan and lurk.

Fefa, they tease,
you cannot see—
how can you climb
the steep steps?
You would fall!

Left behind,
I feel so abandoned,
so ashamed.

Slow Down

I open my blank book
and begin to create
my own fairy-tale world
of dreamlike
words.

I can see the tall
columns of letters
just as long
as I only stare
at one little
part
of
each
word
at
a
time.

Danger

Life changes overnight.
Word-blindness
suddenly feels
like the least
of my troubles.

Papá gathers us
all around him
and delivers
a terrible warning.

No more wandering.
No exploring.
Our whole family
is in danger!
Why?
¡Ay!
Why?

The Danger Chain

Papá explains that when he
and Mamá were young,
armies roamed, and farms
were destroyed by the flames
of war, and innocent families
were herded like cattle,
into camps called leco . . .

My mind fumbles.
I fail to picture
the frightful word . . .

A camp of leconcent . . .

I stop, take a breath,
and think again slowly,
this time in syllables,
starting with *r*,
not *l* . . .
Re—c o n—c e n—t r a—c i ó n.

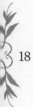

A reconcentration camp.
The tongue-twisting word
finally makes sense.
It was a horrible place
where my poor parents
were fenced in and trapped
during the war years.

Now, Papá explains,
rebellions and chaos
have returned.
Danger roams again,
but this time
the wild men
are not soldiers,
just greedy bandits
who kidnap children
and demand
ransom money.

The wild bandits
were children

during the war years.
They suffered the cruelty
of soldiers.
They learned
how to be cruel.

Danger is a chain,
Papá tells us sadly,
a chain passed from one
wounded child to the next.

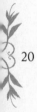

We must stop the danger
by breaking the chain.
We must learn how
to stay safe
and be kind.

Warnings

Be careful, our parents warn us.
Stay away from strangers,
and watch out for kidnappers,
especially the famous ones
like Alvarez and Tolís.
They have already stolen
many children.

All these warnings make me cringe
with dread, but the worst one
is the last one, a dire warning
about ransom . . .

If someone hands me a note,
will I see clearly enough
to read the tricky difference
between friendly words
and a deadly
threat?

Worries

Adjusting to the daily
presence of danger
is a challenge my older
brothers meet
with excitement.

They speak of guns,
knives, and fists.

All I can think of
is learning how
to read
terrifying
ransom notes.

I Do Try!

I obey the new warnings,
along with all our old
family rules.

I am careful, and I work hard
at my chores, tending babies,
drawing water from the well,
plucking beetles out of the beans,
eating carrots for my eyesight,
and picking the smiling faces
of pansies—*pensamiento* flowers,
which are supposed to bring joy
to my thoughts.

I flavor the rice
with fragrant saffron,
and plant longevity flowers
for long life, and pick
the sweet pods
of a candy tree.

23

I help herd cows,
brush horses,
and feed chickens.

The only chore I never
finish is reading
OUT LOUD
to my big sisters,
who laugh
and call me lazy.

I hate hate hate it
when they assume
that I do not
really try.

A Dreaded Gift

On my eleventh Saint's Day
there is candy, coffee, and storytelling,
with everyone interrupting
to ask questions.

There are candles, paper flowers,
and games where the losers
have to do silly things.

I receive a gift that I truly dread,
an album for friends to write in,
giving me poems that I might never
be able to read.

All my big sisters have albums
filled with verses from admirers.
How will I ever manage to read
the sweet poems, if any boy
is ever foolish enough
to admire me?

Imagining

When I ask Mamá why
Santa Mónica has failed
to grant me patience,
she says not to worry,
because now I am eleven,
so I must have at least
eleven thousand invisible
guardian angels, all dancing
on my shoulder.

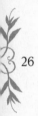

I am afraid that next year,
when twelve thousand
invisible angels
dance beside my ear,
they will just laugh
and mock me,
or get tired
and go to sleep.

Wishing

Is it possible to grow weak
with fear?

All my efforts are failing.
Sometimes I almost feel dizzy,
and even though Mamá insists
that I am just anxious,
I feel absolutely certain
that the scary white pages
in a blank book
can make a word-fearful
eleven-year-old girl
just topple over
and faint.

I wish I knew how
to become word-strong
and word-brave.

Questioning

Some of my brothers and sisters
have such long, complicated names
that I can't write them all,
but I can write the names
of my aunts and uncles,
because there are just a few,
and most of the names are short.

My mother's brothers are Abelino,
Miguel, Arcadio, and Félix.
Her sisters are Ana Luisa,
Sarita, and Leonila.

When all the cousins visit,
the astonishing abundance
of long, complicated names
seems absolutely impossible
to spell correctly,
but I do truly, truly
try!

Fortunately, my favorite
best-friend cousin is Carmen,
with her short, friendly name.

She is the daughter of Tío Miguel
and Tía Lucía, his smiling wife.
Before the wars, Lucía's
African parents were slaves.

My cousin Carmen is free,
but we have to attend different
church schools,
and when we volunteer
to help the nuns
at the convent in town,
Carmen has to enter the church
through a hidden back door.
Why?
¡Ay!
Why?

Bird-People

When I ask Papá to explain,
he says if you don't have blood
from one tribe, you have it
from another—*El que no tiene
sangre del Congo
tiene del Carabalí.*

He tells me that his own
daring Basque ancestors
voyaged to Cuba
by way of Colombia.

Mamá says she is a mixture
of native Cuban *indios*
and musical Canary Islanders,
people who once knew how to talk
like birds, whistling their words.

I am glad to know
that I am part bird-person,

because birds come in all colors,
and they belong to many tribes.
Maybe I should just sing
pretty bird songs at school,
instead of struggling to read
OUT LOUD.

Insults

Rumors of danger fade.
We still have to be careful,
but we no longer stay home.

Reaching the village school
means hitching a wagon to oxen,
or riding a horse, or walking
and walking, until I finally arrive
with red mud on my ankles,
marking me as a *guajira*,
a country girl who has never
ridden in a horseless carriage
or a steaming train.

Stupid *guajira*, the girls taunt,
even though it's not a real village,
just a rickety old sugar mill
where all the other children
are also *guajiros*, part *indio*
and part bird.

Schoolbooks

There are two textbooks.
One is Cuban,
with colorful pictures
of pineapples, parrots,
and ox-carts, ordinary things
that I see each day.

The other book is northern,
with gray drawings
of woolly sheep and snowmen,
strange things that no one
on this tropical island
has ever encountered.

The Cuban book has poems
about jungle flowers
that are like hands
opening in sunlight.
When a flower is closed,
its fist is asleep.

The northern book
has old English poems
about eagles on cold
mountain crags.

I dread both books,
except for the friendly pages
with Cuban *adivinanzas,*
guess-me riddles
like this one:

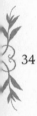

Two girls at a window
tell all without speaking.
Who are they?
Eyes!

If only I could answer
all the questions
in my own life
as easily
as the riddles.

Wildflowers

Town is even farther
than the village.

The streets are cobbled
with smooth, rounded stones.

There are elegant shops,
and an orchestra that plays
in the park, where rich girls
stroll and smile
in pretty clothes.

Every weekend from Lent
until the Feast of San Juan,
guajiro boys gallop into town
with flowers on their saddles.

The country boys toss
wild orchids

to the pretty town girls
in their fancy dresses.

I am sure that no boy
will ever give me flowers.

My dress is too old,
and my eyes are red,
red and swollen
from crying
while I struggle
to write
and read.

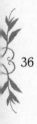

Celebrations

This is the pattern
of each year in the lively town—
contests to see whose caged birds
are the best singers,
then Holy Week, and flowers
for the Virgin of the Sea.
San Juan's Day, San Pedro's Day,
and the feast day of Santiago
on his white ghost horse.
Summer carnival, hurricanes,
yellow clothes for the Virgin
of Charity.
All Saints' Day and the Day
of the Loyal Dead,
Christmas, Three Kings' Day,
Fat Tuesday, Lent,
Palm Sunday, Easter,
and once again, wistful

caged songbird
contests.

This is the pattern of my year
on the farm—find a string,
grasp a crochet hook,
make last year's lacy shawl
a little wider, so it will fit me
like a wraparound wing.

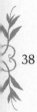

38

I wish the wing-shaped shawl
could carry me away
to any place where no one
would ever ask
if I have finished
my homework.

I gaze at a page.
I am so weary of trying
to fill my blank mind
with wisdom.

I close my schoolbook,
discouraged.
Where does courage go
when it is lost?

Finally, I open my wild book
and write a bold word:
Valentía.
Courage.
Maybe if I claim
my own share of courage
often enough, it will appear.

Imagine the celebration
I will enjoy someday,
if I ever manage
to read one entire book
OUT LOUD!

Word Hunger

Is it possible that I am
no longer completely
discouraged?

I do still dread reading,
but I dread it a little bit less
each day.

When I consider
the happy possibility
that maybe someday
I will feel smart,
I grow a little bit hungry
for small, tasty bites
of easy words.

Word Freedom

My big sisters spy.
They read my wild book.
They laugh and laugh,
because each stream
of rippling words
looks like a crazy poem
that doesn't even
try to rhyme.

Why can't they understand
that rhymes are hard for me
to see and hear?

My drifts of verse
are free words,
wild and flowing.
The world is filled
with things that flow,
like water, feelings,
daydreams, wind . . .

The Ugly Poem

My Saint's Day album has finally
received its first verse!
Fausto the farm manager
is old, but he gives me a poem
that he wrote in my honor.

His handwriting is jagged
and sloppy, but the poem
calls me a rose in a garden.
From now on, should roses
be my favorite flowers?
No!
I will study, so that someday
I can read a lovely poem
from a younger admirer
with graceful handwriting
that does not resemble
the claw marks
of a beast.

Fragrant Chores

I keep thinking about poems
while I work in the kitchen,
making scented decorations.

I pierce oranges with cloves,
sprinkle them with cinnamon,
and set them on the table
in a nest of jasmine petals,
where they look like gold eggs
and smell like perfume.

43

While I do my fragrant chores,
I vow that I will improve
my own handwriting.

I don't want to scrawl words
that look like Fausto's
ugly poem.

Gardens of Thought

When Mamá says go
to the pharmacy, I know
she means the garden,
so I wander past sleepy herbs,
whispery ones, and *mariposas*—
flowers with flute-shaped centers
and outer petals that resemble
butterfly wings.
The wives of rebel soldiers
used to hide secret messages
inside these flowers
during the wars.

While I think of battles
and my own struggle
to read, I begin stringing
a bright necklace
of shiny red and black
chocho seeds,

even though I know
that the prettiest
parts of wild plants
are often the most
poisonous.

Gardens of thought
are not always
peaceful.

Guessing

I memorize all the little
guess-me riddles
in my schoolbook:

> A bird has a little white
> treasure chest
> that everyone knows
> how to open
> but no one can close.
> An egg!

> Why does an unlucky shrimp
> swim backwards?
> To return to a time
> before he lost his luck!

I dream up new riddles
and write them all down
in my wild book.

My slow handwriting
with its careful swirls
and loops
has almost grown
beautiful.

Am I patient?
What has changed?

When I write riddles,
the pen in my hand
feels mysterious.

I feel as powerful
as a girl in a fairy tale,
a brave girl who climbs
dangerous towers
and sips water
from magic wells.

Is this how it feels
to be smart?

Strolling

Rumors of the danger chain
are quiet now, so we enjoy
Sunday outings to town.

After church, I walk
around the lively plaza
with my cousin Carmen.

We are chaperoned
by one of our stern,
black-clad aunts.

Girls promenade
clockwise, while boys strut
counterclockwise.

If a boy makes eye contact
it means he will marry you,
so all the boys are careful,

while the frowning
old chaperones
remain cautious
and wary.

Girls just daydream
and smile.

Towers of Hope

Mamá loves verses
as much as I love
guess-me riddles
and strolling
daydreams.

She loves poetry so much
that she named two
of my little brothers
Rubén and Darío,
after a Nicaraguan poet
who writes about towers
of hope.

When I listen as Mamá reads
OUT LOUD, I imagine
the height of my own
wild hopes.

Growing Up

Sometimes I wonder
if Mamá would have liked
to be a poet, instead
of a farm wife.

When my parents met,
she was only fifteen,
but Papá was all grown up.
He rode by on his horse
and saw her playing a game,
pretending that banana leaves
were a green wedding dress.

He asked her father
for her hand, and soon
they were married.

There were babies,
and more babies,

and then my mother
finally finished
growing up.

I don't want to be married,
with babies and worries,
until I am fully grown.
Even then, I would love
to live without the worries.

I will live far from the farm,
in a city with electricity,
where my husband and I
can dance and stroll
beneath cheerful lights.

I will own at least one
lacy dress with a hem
that is never torn
or muddy.

Ugliness

My brothers interrupt
my daydreams.
They whisper Josefa, Fefa,
Fefa *la fea*.
Fea.
Ugly.
Certain slimy
froglike words
can do a lot more
than jump and tease.

So when a wild parrot
lands on the red tile roof,
I teach it to call out *feo, feo,*
ugly, ugly, hoping
my brothers will understand
that the bright green bird
is talking about them,
not me.

Trouble

Feo, feo.
The chattering parrot
is no longer wild.
It lives on our roof
and calls everyone ugly,
even grownups
and honored guests.

I am in trouble
for teaching insults
to such a smart bird.

While I am in trouble,
I daydream
to keep my thoughts
bright like the parrot,
instead of hideous
like my fears.

54

Uncertainty

I imagine escaping
on Papá's fastest horse.
Where would I go?
To the tower,
just like my sisters.

The tower is on a farm
where long ago,
two wealthy brothers
competed to see who
was stronger.

One built a tower,
and the other dug a well
just as deep as the height
of the tower.

A wandering woman
poured magic into the well,

but she cursed the tower
with evil enchantments,
because it was said
to be used as a watchtower
for catching runaway slaves,
or as a prison tower
for punishing
rebellious wives.

When I daydream,
I feel certain that I will never
marry a man who keeps captives.
But there are so many types
of men, and types of towers—
how will I know?

Can a tower of fear
ever be transformed
into a tower
of hope?

Beastly

When I am finally allowed
out of the house, I walk
down to the green river,
where my brothers
are trying to wrestle
a huge *caimán*
that looks like a crocodile
or a bumpy green dragon
with sharp, vicious teeth.

I wander too close,
and the beast snaps
at my ankle.
One swallow could take
my whole leg!

My brothers shout,
and instantly I know
that they will tell Mamá,

and I will be in trouble
all over again.

I am so scared that later,
when I am alone
with my wild book,
I pay attention
to all the tiniest sounds
as I struggle to write a list
of the long names
of all my beastly
brothers and sisters.

José de Jesús is the oldest.
He swears he will kill
the *caimán*.

Pedro Eulogio brags too,
but Julio Alberto
and Darío Leonelo
are far too young,

and baby Rubén
can't even talk yet.

He just chirps funny tunes
like a new-hatched bird.

Mariana
and María del Carmen
and Juana Quirina
and Leonila Hortensia
and Etelvina María
never brag
about courage
or battling
dragonlike beasts.

All they do is taunt me:
Fefa, Fefa, blind, stupid, *fea* . . .

Tame sisters
can be even crueler
than wild brothers.

Scribbling

Trying to forget my troubles,
I sit alone, jotting another list
of complicated names
in my wild book.

I spell my own long name:
Josefa de la Caridad Uría Peña.

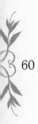

I sound out the name of our farm:
Goatzacoalco.

I pour out the name of the river:
Manatí.

I print the name of the town:
Trinidad.

I whisper the name
of my favorite daydream:
Happiness.

Patience

As soon as I realize
that I have written my own
long name, along with those
of all my brothers and sisters,
I begin to wonder—how
did I learn?

When I write slowly,
learning just seems to grow
out of patience.

The loops of my letters
are almost beautiful!

They look like the tendrils
of a garden vine as it climbs
over a tall fence
to go exploring.

The Hope Bug

School vacation!
Time off.
No dreaded books.
No shameful teasing.
No reading OUT LOUD.

I have time to make jewelry
from the foamy white hearts
of green reeds that I pluck
from the banks of the river.

I have time to weave crickets
from strips of palm leaf.
The crickets are called
esperanzas—hopes.
When I give one to Mamá,
she tells me the little insect
will bring her great luck.
She gives me a hug
in return.

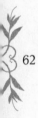

Before the Hunt

Every *caimán* hunt begins
with a huge party.

My father roasts a pig
spiced and wrapped
in banana leaves,
then lowered into a pit
in the deep red soil,
where wood and flames
will transform it
into *un guateque*,
a farmer's feast.

When the cousins arrive,
we start dancing and singing
funny liars' songs.

Later, while boys race horses
and girls cook, cousin Carmen
helps me invent new riddles.

The old folks play dominoes.
Young women fan their faces
while men fight a poetry duel,
battling in powerful voices
to see who can claim
the verse victory,
as each man strives
to recite the most
dramatic
heart-pounding
emotional
poem!

The Poetry Duel

To please my mother,
the poems are Rubén Darío's
verses about swans
and flying horses,
and a strange one about
mental earthquakes,
and an angry poem
for world leaders
who try to bully
the future
with bullets.

There is a drumbeat
verse about loving
your own rhythm

and the encouraging one
about God's towers
of hope

and a joyful little verse
about eggs in a warm nest
in a warm tree.

There is even a poem
that helps me feel normal,
a comforting verse
about feeling blinded
by daydreams.

When Mamá stands up
and recites a LOUD verse—
just like a man—
she chooses the one
about gold seashells
that look like hearts.

That is how I know
that she must be dreaming
of the peaceful beach
where we camp

only once
each summer
even though we live
so close
to the rolling blue sea
that there is nothing
to stop us
from living like mermaids.

We could be discovering
undersea treasures
each day,
gold shells that resemble
wave-washed
hearts.

Fly to the Truth of Dreams

After my mother
finishes her seascape,
one of my uncles recites
a long poem about the sky,
where sun spirits
ride glowing chariots,
and there is someone
who knows how to fly
toward the truth
of dreams . . .

I don't understand
the whole thrilling verse,
but I love the way poetry
turns ordinary words
into winged things
that rise up
and soar!

Rum and Bullets

My big brothers drink rum,
and then, just to frighten me,
they sing an ugly rhyme
about sneaky spiders
and slimy frogs.

They laugh and laugh
while they take turns
admiring a new rifle
that one of our uncles
brought for the hunt.

The rifle is long and shiny.
José de Jesús brags
that the bad *caimán*
does not stand a chance.

He holds the ominous gun
backwards, sideways,
and upside down.

He flips it and spins it,
showing off like a girl
with a fancy new dress.

The rum makes him childish.
The gun makes him dangerous.
He dances a wild rumba,
pretending that the rifle
is his partner.

The explosion
is like nothing
I have ever heard—
thunder and lightning
all rolled into one
stormy burst
of terror.

My brother's eyes
open wide, and then
they slowly sag shut

while my heart flies
rapidly
back and forth
between fear
and grief.

Rum and bullets
are such a deadly
combination.

Why didn't anyone see
that the dragonlike
caimán
was our wild farm's
least dangerous
beast?

Waiting

Patience defies me.
How can I sit quietly
while my brother's life
seeps away?

I tremble and weep
as Mamá binds
the ghastly wound
in a frantic effort
to slow the savage
waterfall
of bleeding.

Papá mounts a horse
and races all the way
to town.

Agonizing hours later,
he finally returns

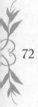

with another
galloping horseman—
the same hissing doctor
who once called me
word-blind.

This time, the doctor
ignores me, working swiftly
to save my brother's life.

All I can do is wait
and watch, hoping
the doctor knows
more about bullets
than blindness.

Discovering My Voice

The parrot on the roof
wails and shrieks, copying
Mamá's desperate prayers
as she begs for a miracle
of healing.

Tear-streaked and silent,
I feel so useless, so helpless—
until an imaginary wild book
opens up, inside my mind.

Quietly, I begin picturing letters,
syllables, and invisible wings,
sending a trail of bird-words
soaring toward heaven.

My silent voice feels
powerful and LOUD.

Ready to Heal

José has survived!
He needs peace and quiet.
I bring him herbs and soup.
I bring him silent smiles.
I receive only frowns
in return.

The doctor advises me
to be patient.
He tells me that my brother
will need plenty of time
to heal.

The doctor's tired voice
no longer sounds like a hiss.

Perhaps my way of hearing
has somehow
changed.

Strange Cures

The bullet missed José's heart,
but it crushed a bone.
His shoulder will always be stiff.
Farm work will be impossible.

Papá tells my brother that he
must find a new way to live.
After a few days of angry
arguments, José announces
that he wants to be a teacher.
He declares that he must begin
by teaching me.

So now I have to read OUT LOUD
while my wounded brother
peacefully listens.

My brother calls it his reading cure.
I call it torture.

Reading Out Loud

I would rather tell riddles
or sing funny liars' songs,
like the one about a spider
who sews clothes for a cricket,
or the one about silly fleas
who wear fancy trousers,
even though they do not
own any underwear at all.

Instead, I have to SOUND OUT
all the difficult syllables
of tiny pieces of long poems
un—til
I am
hope—less—ly
fu—ri—ous—ly
wea—ry.

Fear-Chained

Rumors of danger return,
just when I am already
so exhausted, and all I need
is safety, and all I know
is the possibility of loss.

My brother's wound came
from his own careless
rum-and-rifle dance,
but I cannot help wishing
there were something else
to blame, like *caimáns*
or bandits . . .

As I picture all the links
in life's long chain of dangers,
I grow so anxious that while
my poor brother sleeps
and heals, I begin to scribble

my own oddly
comforting verses,
this growing vine
made of words
that almost sing
but rarely rhyme.

Even scribbling
is such a struggle.

Will my blank book
ever be full?

Wondering

Kidnappers, beasts, bullets . . .
Life seems just as perilous
as during the war years
when my parents
were starving
in a prison camp
and their first baby
died of fever.

I wonder if poor little Haida
is in the air, floating nearby—
perhaps she is one of my
eleven thousand
guardian angels.

Can she hear me trying to cure
my wounded brother
with poems?

Just One

My eyes burn, my head aches,
and my vision feels so weak
that I am afraid to use up
whatever is left of my eyesight.

When I tell José that so much
reading out loud exhausts me,
he advises me to read just one
small part of a single poem
over and over, until I love
the familiar rhythm.

So I choose the Rubén Darío
verse about a blank page,
and I read the same few lines
until I almost begin to feel
calm and safe.

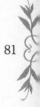

More Practice

José is beginning to seem
like a real teacher.

He encourages me
to practice and practice
more and more,
as if my entire future
depends on nothing
but words.

Maybe
it does.

More and More Poetry

Does one small
accomplishment
always lead to another?

I keep choosing tiny parts
of Rubén Darío's long poems.
There is one about singing leaves,
a magic dragonfly, and birds
of the soul . . .

and another about
a horse that runs
like lightning, moving
as swiftly as an idea . . .

It only takes a few swift lines
to make the rhythmic music
of my imagination
gallop!

The Secret Language
of Children

When she thinks I need a rest,
Mamá sends me to the garden
to gather *manzanilla* flowers
for a soothing tea to help
baby Rubén fall asleep.

I return to the porch and find
José playing a foolish game
with little Julio and Etelvina,
a game called *jerigonzas*—
nonsense—also known
as the secret language
of Cuban children.

I have never mastered the art
of making sense from nonsense.

José tries to coach me.
Take any word.
Add *chi* after each syllable.
If grownups can still
understand, try *chiri*
instead of *chi.*

Etelvina has no trouble
turning Fefa into Fechifachi,
and Julio is clever enough
to lengthen Fefa
into Fechirifachiri.

All I manage to do is end up
feeling like a long riddle
without any answer.

Never Give Up

I practice and practice,
until I finally do
manage to hear
the tricky syllables
of hi—lar—i—ous
ri—dic—u—lous
make-believe
nonsense words.

If only the rest
of my strange life
made as much sense
as nonsense.

Never give up,
my brother advises.
Never.
Nevchierchi.
Nevchirierchiri.

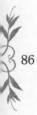

Hideous

Just when I've started feeling
safe and smart, the farm manager
bothers me with ugly questions.
Do I like the verse he wrote
in my album?
Has anyone else given me
a rhyme?
Have young boys ever called me
a rose?
Would I like another poem,
and maybe a kiss . . .

I am so alarmed, and so ashamed
that I tell no one, not even José,
not even in our language
of secrets.

Danger Grows

My father has finally killed
the dangerous *caimán*
that caused so much trouble.
Our river would be safe now
if there weren't so many
new reports of farm children
kidnapped by the bandits
Alvarez and Tolís.
So Papá gives Fausto a pistol
and tells him to guard us,
protect us, keep us all safe . . .

Guns in the hand
of a tricky man?
Certain ordinary words
crowded so close together
make no sense at all.

I am not brave enough
to protest.

Sleepless

No matter how long
and tangled the danger chain
grows, I still have to cook
a hearty lunch of meat,
rice, beans, yams, coffee,
wild fruit, and pudding.

Afterward, during the quiet
siesta hour, when we are all
supposed to sleep, I sit up
and sway in a rocking chair,
wondering, worrying . . .

Did anyone hear Fausto's
hideous questions?

Will I be blamed
for his ugly words?

A Laughter Gift

I hardly ever smile anymore,
but when three of my oldest,
most shriveled great-aunts
come to visit, they bring
a gift of humor.

Seated in rocking chairs
on the porch, they grin
and wave at three gallant
young horsemen
who prance by, hoping
to flirt with three
of my prettiest big sisters.

At the sight of old women
beckoning, the boys gallop away
so swiftly that they don't have
a chance to hear me
join my mischievous

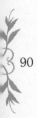

old aunts'
chuckles
and giggles
and guffaws
of amusement.

Surrounded by laughter,
I almost feel safe.

Daily Music

During perilous times
we rarely feast,
but my brothers
still perform rope tricks
that look
like a ballet
of the leaping horse
and looping rope,
and my sisters
stir a coconut pudding
that sounds like a rumba
of the kettle
and the spoon.

I compete with José
to see who can sing
the best liars' song.

He invents one about cows
that give sweet, delicious

whipped cream
instead of plain milk.

I sing about an earthworm
that wears a fancy hat,
even though he does not
have a head.

After a few funny songs,
any starlit evening
can turn into a lively
family dance.

Dance-Smart

Everyone says I am
a fine dancer!
Suddenly, I feel drumbeat,
guitar-ripple, maraca-rattle
dance-smart.

José is a naturally
smart teacher,
and Darío has a way
with plants in the garden,
and baby Rubén
or little Etelvina
might grow up to be smart
in the handy way of artists,
carving statues
or painting murals.

I am dance-smart
when my feet

and hands

forget to worry

about the rhythms

that I know

how to tap

and clap

OUT LOUD.

Still Struggling

As soon as I touch
my wild book
with dancing fingers,
I have to start all over,
re—mem—ber—ing
to
move
oh
so
slowly,
writing
a graceful,
patient
waltz,
not
a rapidly
pounding
conga.

Storytelling

No one in my family
ever throws anything away,
not even an old story
that can be told and retold
late at night, to make the deep
darkness feel
a little less lonely.

In the garden, there is a vine
with fragrant white flowers.
Long ago, it was an Indian girl
who was forced to flee
from Spanish soldiers.
She hid alone in the forest
and learned the language
of animals—
as soldiers approached,
she turned into a flower,

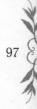

but all the animals
still know her.

When our little farm dog
sniffs the fragrant vine,
I imagine he must be talking
to the frightened girl.

Back in the time
when stories were born,
the entire island of Cuba
was covered with an immense
ancient forest.

Now, the towering trees
are mostly gone, replaced
by rolling hills
and open pastures.

If dangerous men
ever chase me,
where will I hide?

One Strand at a Time

When an uncle brings piles
of the white cotton strings
and green silk threads
that are used for tying
cement sacks, my mother
crochets a lovely white purse.

She gives me the green silk
to make a shimmering
winglike shawl.

My hands fly one loop
at a time, like dancing doves
in an emerald sky, scribbling
mysterious bird-words.

I feel like a girl in a story,
human and magical
at the same time.

The Beach in August

The cows are fat, and Papá
is ready for a vacation.
He trusts Fausto
to take care of the farm.

We pack our white dresses
and wide straw hats.
Mamá is so excited that she sings,
Get this, get that, hurry up . . .

Everything we own
seems to be going with us
to our sandy camping place
at the seashore.

The beach is not far away,
but the journey takes us
through a murky marsh,
past manatees

that look like smiling
chubby mermaids.

I wonder if the gentle manatees
know that *caimáns*, crocodiles,
and sharks
all lurk beneath the surface,
watching and waiting . . .

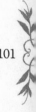

The Beach at Noon

Too much sun, too much sand.
Stingrays, jellyfish, spiny
purple urchins that pierce
my careless feet . . .

We eat so much fish
that I expect to sprout
shiny fins and a glistening
green tail.

I am tired of drinking
nothing but coconut milk,
tired of cracking crab claws,
tired of brothers throwing sand
and sisters teasing.

Papá says it doesn't matter,
as long as the whole family
is together.

The Beach at Night

Everything glows.
The sky is made of stars
and the waves are
phosphorescent.
Phos—pho—res—cent.

I sound out syllables,
even though here
at the peaceful beach
I don't have to read,
scribble, or do anything
but slow down and listen
to the natural poem-songs
whistled and whooshed
by water, birds, wind,
and the coiled tunnels
hidden in trumpet-shaped
seashells.

Storm

Disappointing news—
we have to leave
the windy beach now,
right now . . .

A whirling hurricane
looms
offshore.

I am ready to flee,
but at first, Mamá refuses.
All she wants to do
is swim and sigh,
burying her fingers
in hot, salty sand.

I think she must be
part mermaid
or part poet.

Home

Our green farm looks
so welcoming and friendly
that I am even happy to see
the messy red mud,
but as we get closer,
something begins to feel
dangerous.
Cows are tied to trees,
as if ready for a journey
of their own.
Thieves!

My brothers shout
and my father curses.
It is clear that the cattle
are tied up so that they
can be stolen.

Home is no longer
a place to feel safe.

Awake All Night

The rustlers gallop away
before my brothers
can catch them.

They did not get our cows,
but they took my ability
to sleep.

I lie awake, listening
to the beastly shrieks
and roars
of hurricane wind.

How can nighttime
be filled with so many
terrifying daydreams?

Reading Wildly

I get up and wander
with a candle in my hand,
the light a bright flicker
of comfort.

On the kitchen table
I find a piece of paper
with squiggly letters.
I struggle to con—cen—trate,
peering and squinting,
telling myself that I am not
word-blind.

I can read, eagerly,
sss—low—lll—yyy,
carefully, even though
I feel like a fat manatee
swimming away
from sleek sharks.

Ghostly

The paper is ugly,
a hideous, horrible
ransom note.
Oh.
¡Ay!
Why?
No!
It is my worst fear,
signed by the two
infamous kidnappers,
Alvarez and Tolís.

I am furious, confused.
The eerie note haunts me.
The bold, sloppy writing
looks ghostly as it shrieks:
PAY
OR LOSE
YOUR CHILDREN.

Doomed

I stare at the threat,
feeling certain that I've seen
this jagged, knife-blade shred
of ugly handwriting before
somewhere else, long ago
in a nightmare . . .

Papá is behind me now,
grumbling and muttering
something about having
so many children that he
could never hope to pay
a ransom for all . . .

What will become
of us?

I feel as lost as the girl
who turned into a flower,

only I am just one
detached
windblown
petal,
weightless
and rootless.

Even the presence
of my sturdy father
is not enough
to help me feel
like a natural plant
with a place
to belong.

Thorns

José saddles his horse
to ride into town for help.
His shoulder aches, but he
refuses to stand around
feeling helpless.

I have no choice.
I am just a useless child,
who cannot even
make sense
of a ransom note's
ugliness.

I stare at the note,
but I feel just like I did
months ago, when words
still jumped and slithered
like restless green frogs
or slippery striped snakes.

Then I see it,
the nightmarish
connection—
this tilted, angry,
hideous handwriting
must be Fausto's.

In my album, the ugly poem
spoke of a rose in a garden.

Now I see it so clearly.
Here are the thorns.

Flying

So I fetch my album,
and I show the ugly verse
to my father.

I tell what I know.
I fly to the truth of words.

Outraged, Papá shudders,
then promises to remedy
all that is wrong.

Flying to the truth of words
instantly helps me
feel
as secure
as a flower
with deep roots.

Justice

Men in uniforms gallop
to the farm.

Fausto tries to escape,
but he ends up with his wrists
trapped in handcuffs—
he is the captive,
not me.

114

Our family is safe.
Papá calls me a heroine.
Mamá calls me an angel.
José tells me that I am
the slowest, most careful,
observant reader
he has ever known.

I have finally received
encouragement
from a teacher.

Blank

Once the crisis is over
and we have been rescued,
I tear up the ugly poem's
ragged words, destroying
this thorny feeling
of shame.

My album
is empty.

At first
the white pages
seem lonely,

but after a few minutes
the blankness looks sunlit,

like clear blue sky
after a storm.

Surprises

I never expected a reward,
but Mamá is making a lacy
blue dress that I can wear
to Carmen's Saint's Day feast,
and Papá has given me
the gift of his trust.

José offers to take me
on an adventurous outing,
all the way to the tower.

He is seated proudly
on a coppery horse,
but he says that I
am too old to ride
like a boy.

I have to sit sideways
on a spotted mare,

wishing that horses
were not quite
so tall.

There is nothing
like a sidesaddle
to test a young girl's
courage.

I wonder how many
men could keep their balance
in such a precarious position.
Pre—car—i—ous.

Women have no choice.
We grow accustomed
to sitting sideways,
seeing only half
of the dangerous road
up ahead.

Inside the Tower of Fear

My brother stays
with the horses
while I climb
and climb
and climb.

Darkness—
a steep
stairway
of splintered
rotting wood.

On the fifth story
I feel dizzy.

By the sixth
I am exhausted.

On the seventh
there are small

118

welcoming windows
bright with sun.

I lean out
and dare myself
to enjoy
the wide view
of green hills,
blue sea,
and a sky
so enormous
and peaceful
that I don't have to
actually see
all my thousands
of guardian angels
to believe that they
are watching me.

Magic

When I finally
climb back down
from the tower,
I sip a bit of water
from the well.

I don't really feel
any different, but it's easy
to imagine that today
I have grown
just a little bit
stronger
and wiser.

Courage

This is the last
blank page.

My wild book is full.
I am surprised to discover
that I can no longer bear
the thought of an entire day
without the natural flow
of twining
vinelike words . . .

So I pick up one
of the thick books
I used to hate, and I open
its gate-shaped cover,
and I let my strong eyes
travel,
slowly
exploring.

Author's Note

The Wild Book is fiction inspired by stories my maternal grandmother told me about her childhood. I have added numerous imaginary aspects, and certain events have been altered or condensed in time. For instance, baby Rubén was not born until 1914.

Josefa de la Caridad Uría Peña was known to all who loved her as Fefa. Born in 1901, she grew up on a farm during the chaos following Cuba's wars for independence from Spain and the subsequent U.S. occupation of the island. It was a time of lawlessness, when bandits terrorized the countryside, kidnapping children unless their families agreed to deliver ransom money in advance. It was also a time when poetry was a treasured aspect of daily life. The kidnapper-poet who threatened the Uría family was their trusted farm manager. Well past the age of one hundred, my grandmother still remembered the verse he wrote "in her honor":

Al verla tan jovencita
y de tanta educación
le busco la proporción
que busco entre las demás
y en este jardin será
una rosa de Borbón.

Seeing her so young
and so accomplished,
I seek a measure
of her place among others,
and in this garden she will be
a rose of Borbón.

My grandmother always chuckled when she told
the story of her father's reaction to the scoundrel's
threat. My great-grandfather said he had too many
children to pay a ransom for all, and since he be-
lieved in equality, he refused to choose favorites.
Rather than pay for some, he paid for none. Fortunately, Fausto was caught and went to prison before any of the children were actually kidnapped.

Fefa (upper right) at a picnic with her family in 1914.

Word-blindness was a medical term used in the early twentieth century for what we now call dyslexia, a range of conditions now known to be completely unrelated to any form of blindness. With patience, courage, and the help of reading specialists, dyslexic children learn to read and write beautifully. Many are exceptionally brilliant people who go on to accomplish great things. Throughout her remarkably long life, Fefa always wrote letters to her loved ones. She wrote slowly and carefully. She had the most elegant handwriting I have ever seen.

Acknowledgments

I thank God for blank pages.

I am profoundly grateful to my *abuelita* for telling me stories about her childhood, and to my daughter, Nicole, for asking me to give her great-grandmother's life a home on blank pages. I am thankful to my mother for filling in factual details and then allowing me to change them.

For the encouragement of companionship, special thanks to Curtis, Victor, Kristan, Jake, Nicole, and Amish.

Gracias a los primos for leading the way up the steep stairs of La Torre Manaca-Iznaga.

For help with my humbling effort to understand even a tiny fragment of the complexity of reading disorders, I am thankful to Jossie O'Neill, the International Dyslexia Association, the Dyslexia Foundation, and LD Online. Any errors in my portrayal of reading disorders are mine, not theirs.

For wonderful teamwork, I am deeply grateful

to my brilliant editor, Reka Simonsen, and to ev-
eryone else at Harcourt, especially Betsy Groban,
Jeannette Larson, Lisa DiSarro, Adah Nuchi, and
Kerry Martin.

PHOTO © MARSHALL W. JOHNSON

MARGARITA ENGLE is a Cuban American poet and novelist whose work has been published in many countries. Her books include *The Surrender Tree*, a Newbery Honor book and winner of the Pura Belpré Award, the Jane Addams Children's Book Award, the Américas Award, and the Claudia Lewis Poetry Award; *The Poet Slave of Cuba*, winner of the Pura Belpré Award and the Américas Award; *Tropical Secrets; The Firefly Letters;* and *Hurricane Dancers.* She lives with her husband in Northern California.